Paws Goes To The Library

Juliette Goodrich

Illustrations by Susan Shorter

AuthorHouse™
1663 Liberty Drive
Bloomington, IN 47403
www.authorhouse.com
Phone: 1-800-839-8640

Published by AuthorHouse 03/08/2013

ISBN: 978-1-4817-1919-3 (sc)
*   978-1-4817-1920-9 (e)*

Library of Congress Control Number: 2013903597

Any people depicted in stock imagery provided by Thinkstock are models,
and such images are being used for illustrative purposes only.
Certain stock imagery © Thinkstock.

This book is printed on acid-free paper.

authorHOUSE®

Dedication & Acknowledgments:

Dedicated to My Three Children:
Taylor, Kendall and Cameron and all the young readers in the
world !

And special acknowledgments to The Pleasanton Library Paws to
Read Program and The Valley Humane Society and its furry friends
and volunteers.

Paws Goes To The Library

When I was a pup I was nicknamed Paws
You see I was born with these GY- NORMOUS flaws

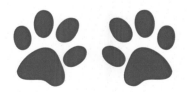

My real name is Rocky but no one calls me by name

Whenever friends want to play.... It's the make fun of my paws game.

"Hey Big Foot!" or "Hey Big Paws" "Go Fetch The Ball"

My feelings get a little hurt but I still answer their call.

But one day I decided I was going to change my look.

So I went to the library to check out a book.

I wanted to find a way to make my paws cute and small.

There must be a magic paw doctor that I can call.

During my visit to the library something caught my eye.

It was a little boy reading to his mom.

She kept saying, "Just try."

Just try what? I wondered as I walked on by.

The boy looked so sweet but he had a tear falling from his eye.

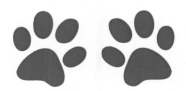

He looked up and saw me gazing his way...

"Momma," the boy said, "can I stop reading and go play?"

"No, Sammy," she said "You need to keep practicing to read.

All the other kids in your class are picking up speed."

"Oh mom, it's so hard for me. I don't know why.

I get so sad because I try and try and try."

All of a sudden my worries about my paws slipped my mind.

I wanted to help Sammy. "Oh what fun book can I find?"

Awww... this one looks good. It's about furry friends at the zoo.

It has colorful pictures and lots of words to read too!

I put the book between my paws and dropped it by Sammy's feet.

"Will you read to me?" I asked, "that would be such a treat!"

The boy's mom looked up and started to smile

"I think Sammy would love to read to you, please stay for awhile."

Sammy opened the book and started to sound out each letter.

And the more pages he read he got better and better.

I cuddled up to listen to the words Sammy read.

But more special to me was where he rested his head.

He was so comfy cozy on my furry paws.

For the first time in my doggie life I had no flaws!!!!!!!

Sammy felt at ease as he kept reading away.
And something special occurred to me on this library day.
Sammy didn't care if my paws were GY-NORMOUS and funny.
He just liked having a friend to read to and liked petting my tummy.

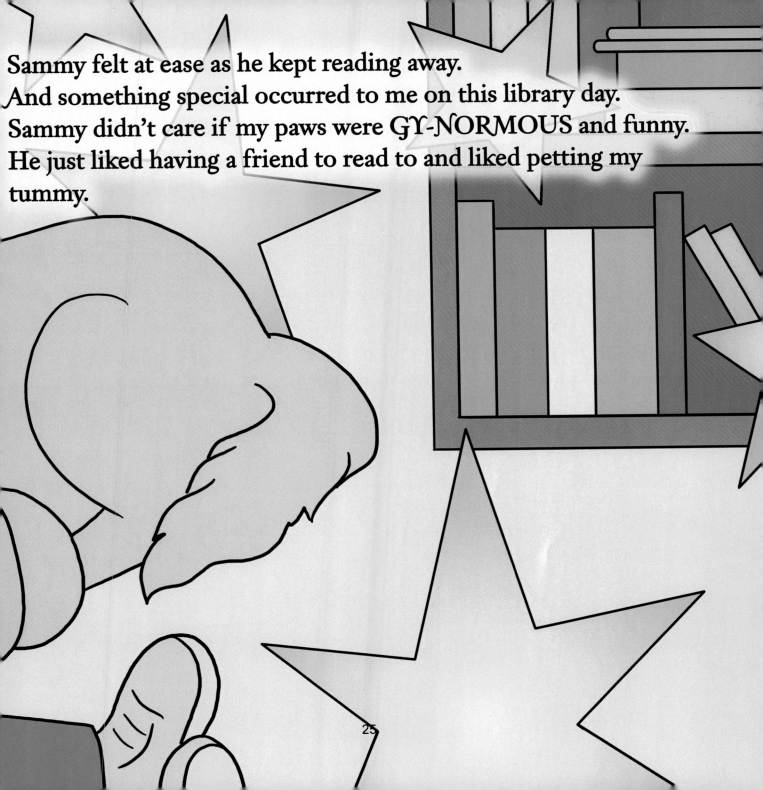

We decided to meet at the library once a week.

Sammy would read out loud and I would listen since dogs really can't speak.

When my pup friends found out about Sammy and me.

They couldn't wait to visit the library.

Sammy invited some of his friends too.

And that's how it all began... a reading dream come true!!!

Books and more books being passed all around.

Dogs curling up sweetly not making a sound.

Sammy of course always picked me.

He loved resting his head on my paws and reading quietly.

34

One day Sammy's mom showed me a note.

It was from Sammy's teacher. Here is what she wrote.

"Sammy's reading skills have put him at the top of the school.

Please thank his furry friends for making reading so cool!"

WHAT IS YOUR FAVORITE BOOK TO READ?

37

IF YOU WERE TO WRITE A STORY BOOK
WHAT WOULD IT BE ABOUT?

42

Pleasanton Public Library Paws to Read Program

The **Pleasanton Public Library** is a municipal library located in the San Francisco Bay Area. The library is a vibrant and integral part of the city of Pleasanton, serving a population of approximately 71, 000. Not only is it a place for disseminating information, but it also serves as a popular social venue for special interest groups, adults, teenagers and children.

The Pleasanton Public Library is proud to be the first library in California to provide *Paws to Read*, an innovative and valuable program that partners the library with Valley Humane Society's Canine Comfort pet therapy volunteers. Since November 2002, this unique program has paired children, dogs and their handlers in an environment that is nurturing and supportive. The fun, non-judgmental experience affords children an opportunity to gain confidence and improve reading skills when sharing books with enthusiastic canine listeners.

The Pleasanton Public Library is an especially popular destination for first through fifth graders attending the *Paws to Read* program on Tuesday evenings. This much-in-demand program is offered for six consecutive weeks during the fall, winter, and spring as well as for four weeks in the summer. There are two 25 minute reading sessions each evening. Between 18 and 22 handlers together with their dogs participate each week. In partnership with local schools, reading specialists are given priority registration for their students. Once open to the public this program usually fills within a few hours. Those children who are not formally registered are encouraged to come to the library on the night of the program and add their names to a drop-in waiting list.

Paws to Read has inspired many local and national libraries to implement similar programs. For the past three years some of the *Paws to Read* volunteers have also been visiting a special day class at one of the local elementary schools. The Pleasanton Public Library looks for innovative ways to expand this transformative program.

For more information:

Pleasanton Public Library
400 Old Bernal Ave
Pleasanton, CA 94566
(925) 931-3400 ext. 8
www.ci.pleasanton.ca.us/library.html

About Valley Humane Society

VALLEY HUMANE SOCIETY (VHS) has been part of the Tri-Valley community since 1987, working to create a brighter future for cats and dogs by encouraging and strengthening the bond between people and pets. VHS rescues and rehabilitates companion animals, champions responsible caretaking through humane education, and preserves existing pet-guardian relationships.

As part of Valley Humane Society's Canine Comfort pet therapy program, *Paws to Read* was developed in partnership with the Pleasanton Public Library by a VHS volunteer who worked for the library. In addition to helping children improve their reading skills, our dog/guardian teams visit rehabilitation units, veteran's hospitals, senior centers, and more, to share the soothing affections of pets with those who need it most. Canine Comfort pet therapy teams are comprised of community volunteers who desire to make a difference in the lives of others, together with their personal pets. Each dog must undergo a behavioral evaluation and health certification to participate.

Valley Humane Society can achieve our vision of a world in which every animal is loved and every person knows the love of an animal by working hand in hand with the community, bringing together compassionate, dedicated people for the good of all. Whether you'd like to adopt an animal, share your passion for pets, or meet like-minded people, VHS is *Your Means to a Friend*™. We invite you to join us!

FOR MORE INFORMATION:

Valley Humane Society
3670 Nevada Street
Pleasanton, CA 94566
(925) 426-8656
www.valleyhumane.org